Tried and Tested Assessment Pack 6

Contents

Introduction

▼ This booklet contains seven assessments that allow teachers to easily determine the extent to which key mathematical skills have been mastered by Sixth Class pupils.

▼ Assessment can help the teacher and the child in a number of different ways. Firstly, it can show how the children are progressing in the different strands of the curriculum, providing a basis for future planning in those areas. Secondly, it can help in the pacing of work by indicating the strengths and weaknesses of a particular group, and lastly, it can play a diagnostic role in identifying particular areas of difficulty for a child.

Key Features

▼ Included among the new and exciting features are:

Fifth Class Skills

- A **Beginning of Year Assessment** based on Fifth Class Skills that will quickly identify each pupil's strengths and weaknesses as they begin the Sixth Class programme, thereby facilitating early **planning and intervention** by the teacher. The Fifth Class skills are listed in the Solutions Book.

Sixth Class Skills

- Four other assessments will enable the teacher to **track each pupil's progress** on an ongoing basis throughout the year.
- The **End of Year Assessment** on pages 29 – 35 will serve as a comprehensive guide to the overall progress of each pupil throughout the year.
- These five assessments are designed to test the pupil's **mastery of the 70 key skills**, which are outlined in the revised curriculum for Sixth Class. The Sixth Class skills are also listed in the **Solutions Book.**
- Some of the **numeracy skills are retested**, reflecting the importance of giving pupils several opportunities to master those particular skills. For example, the problem-solving skills involving addition, subtraction, multiplication and division are tested in each of the five assessments.

▼ There is a great emphasis in the revised mathematics curriculum on the pupil's ability to perform simple mental calculations. Due to the introduction of calculators in Fourth Class, it is important at this stage to measure the extent of pupils' ability to work out the answers to relatively easy questions in their heads – without the help of either paper or calculators. To that end, a Mental Assessment is provided on pages 23 – 28.

Beginning of Year Assessment*

Part One

Tests Fifth Class Skills

1. Show 101.06 on this abacus picture.

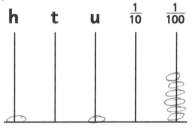

2. Write down the number shown on this abacus picture.

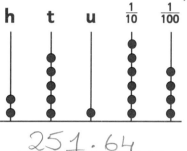

   251.64

3. Write out these numbers in order, starting with the largest.
   245.375, 254.735, 245.575   254.735 , 245.575 , 245.375

4. Round 4349 to the nearest hundred. 4340

5. Round 19.424 to the nearest whole number. _____

6. 7.834 + 15.176 = _____

7. 12.65 – 6.875 = _____

8. 6 x 14.284 = _____

9. 962 ÷ 26 = _____

10. 716.58 ÷ 9 = _____

    $27\overline{)945}$ 94
    0 31·6

11. 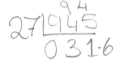 This packet contains 27 biscuits. How many full packets can be made from 945 biscuits? 31.6

12. $\frac{5}{8}$ = $\frac{10}{}$

13. Put these fractions in order, starting with the largest.
    $\frac{5}{9}$, $\frac{2}{3}$, $\frac{1}{6}$ _____, _____, _____

14. Write $\frac{29}{100}$ in decimal form. _____

15. Write $\frac{29}{8}$ as a mixed number. _____

16. Write $4\frac{5}{6}$ as an improper fraction. _____

---

* Note to teacher: The questions in this assessment match the Fifth Class skills 1–63, i.e. Question 1 tests Skill 1, Question 2 tests Skill 2 and so on.

17. Write in $\frac{5}{9}$ in the correct place on this part of the number line.

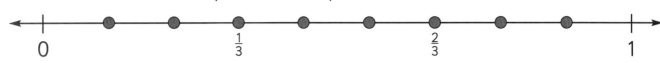

0        $\frac{1}{3}$ $\frac{2}{3}$ 1

18. $2\frac{5}{6} + 3\frac{2}{3} = $ _____   19. $6\frac{3}{8} - 2\frac{3}{4} = $ _____   20. $6 \times \frac{7}{12} = $ _____

21. $70\% = $ _____ . _____   22. $\frac{3}{5} = $ _____ %

23. Write these amounts in order, starting with the smallest.
$\frac{3}{10}$, 0.4, 35% _____, _____, _____

24. Write in 75% in the correct place on this part of the number line.

$\frac{4}{6}$
$\frac{9}{10}$

0        $\frac{1}{8}$ 0.5   1

25. Find 80% of €480. €96 _____

$5\overline{)480}$
0 9 6

26.  This is 60% of Seán's money.
How much money does he have? _____

27. Write the prime number that is greater than 20 and less than 28. _____

28. Write the composite number that is bigger than 4 and less than 8. _____

29. How many square numbers are there between 20 and 30? _____

30. Tick the box that shows the missing number in this sentence.
'The number 12 can have one ☐ two ☐ three ☐ rectangular shapes.'

31. F30 = (_____)

32. 21, 28, 35 are multiples of _____.   Part One: Skills mastered ◻ 32

2

33. Last Sunday morning the temperature in New York was 9°C. By midnight it had dropped by 15°C. What was the temperature at midnight? _-6°C_

34. (28 + 37) ÷ 5 − 8 = _5_

35. Write a word story to match this number sentence and find the answer.

8 x 4 = ☐ _____

_____

36.  Write a number sentence to match this word story. There are 48 children in the 2 Fifth Classes in St John's National School. The principal divided them into groups of 6. How many groups were there altogether? _48÷6=_

37. Find the missing number. 3 x ☐9 = 27

38. An isosceles triangle has 2 _____ sides.

39. Name the quadrilateral that has 4 equal sides, 2 acute angles and 2 obtuse angles. _____

40. Draw a radius in this circle.

41. In this box draw a circle with a diameter of 6cm.

42. Name the 3-D shape that has 5 triangular faces and 1 pentagonal face.

_____

43. Draw the net of a cylinder in this box.

44. Shade the acute angle in this quadrilateral.

45. 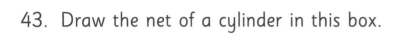 Measure this angle using a protractor. ∠A = _____°

46. Using a ruler, pencil and a protractor, draw an angle that measures 60° in this box.

47. Calculate the size of angle A in this triangle without using a protractor. _____°

48. _____ Measure the length of this line. _____cm

49. Find the length of the perimeter of this shape. _____cm

50. Find the width of this rectangle. _____cm

Area = 8cm²

4cm

51. 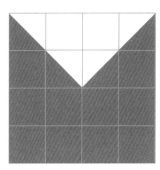 Find the area of the coloured shape. ____cm²

52. Calculate the area of this shape. ____cm²

8cm

4cm

53.

News	12:55
Weather	13:09
Open House	13:14

How long did the news last? 14/19 minutes

54. Write 6:15 p.m. in 24-hour time. 18:15pm.

55.  Which is better value: 6 oranges for €1.50 or 10 oranges for €2.60? 10 oranges =€0.26c ea

6)1.50   10)2.60
0.25   0.26

56. Michelle's mother works in an office. She works Monday to Friday and earns €72 a day. How much does she earn in a week? €360

'72
X5
€360

57.

No.	Item	Each	Total
2	Milk	60c	€1.20
3	Yoghurt	35c	€1.05
4	Apples	25c	€1.00
		Total:	€3.25

Find the total cost of the items in this shopping list.

'35
X3
105

225
X4
100

58.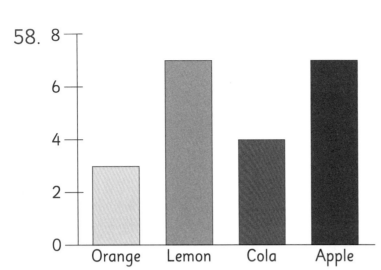

This bar chart shows the favourite drinks of the children in Fifth Class in Glenside National School. 2 children were absent the day the children were surveyed. How many children are there altogether in the Fifth Class when all are present? _23_

14
17
21

59. This pie chart shows how Millside Rovers did in the league last season. They played 30 games altogether. How many games did they win? _20_

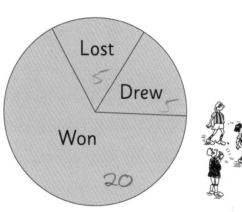

60.

Day	Mon	Tue	Wed	Thurs	Fri	Sat	Sun
Mins	21	28	29	30	40	59	38

49   59   99   38

This table shows the amount of time that Aoife spent watching TV each day last week.

On average, how much time did she spend watching TV each day? _____

61. Based on the table above, on how many days did Aoife spend longer than average watching TV? _245mins_

62. Circle the total that is not possible when 2 dice are thrown together.
2, 5, 7, 13, 4, 6

6

63. Tomorrow Michael has 3 tests to do in school. He wants to do well in all 3 tests.

Number the following sentences in the order that you think Michael is likely to behave tonight. Begin with the most likely as number 1 and so on.

4 Michael will stay out playing with his friends until 10 o'clock.

1 He will spend 2 hours preparing for the tests.

2 He will study for an hour and then watch TV for the rest of the evening.

3 He will spend 20 minutes studying and then go to the cinema with his best friend.

1. $3375 \div 27 =$ _____ **S8**

2. Find the missing number. $\dfrac{}{3} = \dfrac{8}{12}$ **S11**

3. Put these fractions in order, beginning with the largest.

   $\dfrac{7}{10}$, $\dfrac{1}{2}$, $\dfrac{4}{5}$, ____, ____, ____ **S12**

4. Write $\dfrac{38}{100}$ as a decimal. _____ **S13**

5. Write $\dfrac{19}{7}$ as a mixed number. _____ **S14**

6. Change $2\frac{3}{4}$ to an improper fraction. _____ **S15**

7. Place $\dfrac{4}{5}$ in the correct place on this part of the number line.

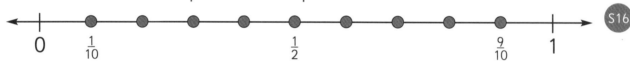 **S16**

8. Express 10 as a fraction of 15. _____ **S17**

9. $2\frac{3}{5} + 1\frac{7}{10} =$ ____ **S18**   10. $3\frac{2}{3} - 1\frac{5}{6} =$ ____ **S19**

11. Circle the prime number in this list. 6, 7, 9, 10, 12 **S27**

12. Circle the composite number in this list. 13, 16, 17, 19, 23 **S28**

13. 1 is the first square number. Write down the fourth square number. ____ **S29**

14. Write down the highest common factor of 21 and 35. _____ **S30**

15. Find the lowest common multiple of 12 and 15. _____

16. $\sqrt{49}$ = _____

17. True or false? Tick the correct box. $16 = 4^2$ T ☐ F ☐ S33

18. Use one of the following words to describe this angle: acute, obtuse, reflex, right, straight. _____ angle S47

19.  Use your protractor to measure this angle. _____° S48

20. In this box, construct an angle that measures 150°. S49

21. Calculate the size of angle D without using a protractor.

   ∠D = _____° S50

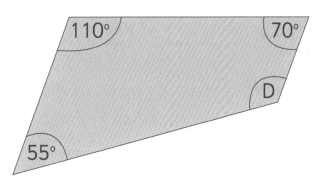

You may use a calculator for Questions 22 and 23.

22. Convert €25 to sterling.

   £_____ sterling

23. What is US$190 worth in euro?

   €_____

Euro Exchange Rates	
Currency	Euro value
Sterling	0.66
US dollar	0.95

Number of skills mastered ⧄ 23

1. Show 26.073 on this abacus.

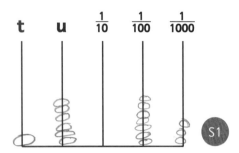

S1

2. Write the number shown on this abacus.

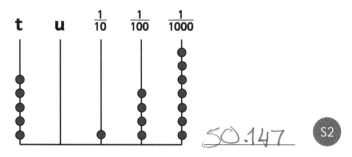

50.147 S2

3. Put these numbers in order, starting with the smallest.
123.761, 123.176, 123.617 _____, _____, _____ S3

4. Round 84.457 to 2 decimal places. _____ S4

5. 19.637 + 126.568 = _____ S5

6. 37.13 – 18.496 = _____ S6

7. 2987 ÷ 29 = _____ S8

8. Alan has saved 3 times as much as his sister Siobhán. Alan has saved €73.80. How much has Siobhán saved? €24.60 S10

3|73.80
24.60

9. $\frac{18}{4}$ = 4 $\frac{2}{4}$ S14

10. 2$\frac{2}{5}$ = $\frac{12}{5}$ S15

11. Write $\frac{5}{6}$ in the correct place on this part of the number line.

S16

0        $\frac{1}{3}$ 1

12. 8 is ☐ of 40. S17

13. $\frac{3}{8} + \frac{3}{4}$ = ___ ☐ S18

14. $\frac{4}{5} - \frac{3}{10}$ = ☐ S19

15. 45% = ___.___ S23

16. $\frac{1}{8}$ = ___% S24

10

17. By how much is 25% of 96 greater than 20% of 115? _____

18. Circle the prime number in this list. 34, 35, 36, 37, 38, 39

19. List the common factors of 12 and 20. _____

20. Find the lowest common multiple of 6 and 9. ____

21. $\sqrt{81}$ = ____ S32

22. Write ⁻3 in the correct place on this part of the number line.

23. ⁻7 + ⁺3 = ‾4 S35

24. Each angle in an equilateral triangle measures _____°. S39

25. True or false? Tick the correct box.
    All quadrilaterals have 2 acute and 2 obtuse angles. T ☐ F ☐ S40

26. In the box, construct a triangle in which
    2 of the angles measure 90° and 45° and
    1 side measures 4cm. S41

27. Draw in and shade a sector in this circle. S42

28. In this box, construct a circle with a diameter of 4cm.

29.  Colour the obtuse angle in this shape.

30. Use a protractor to measure this angle. $\angle A =$ _____°

31. In this box, construct an angle of 95°.

32. 708m = ___._____km

33. 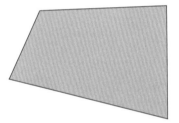 Measure the perimeter of this shape. _____cm

34. This is a scale drawing of an atlas. How wide is the atlas in reality? _____cm

1:5

You may use a calculator for Questions 35 and 36.

35. €6 = US$_____

36. £2.72 sterling = €_____

Euro Exchange Rates	
Currency	Euro value
Sterling	0.68
US dollar	0.98

37. This trend graph shows the number of bicycles sold in a sports shop over the first six months of a year.

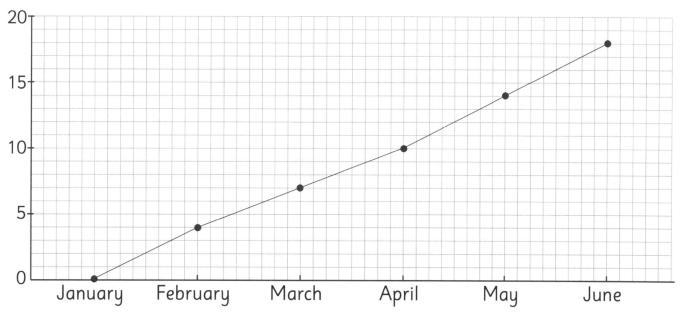

How many more bicycles were sold between April and June than between January and March? _____ S64

$\cancel{2}00$
30
$\overline{1\ 70}$

38.

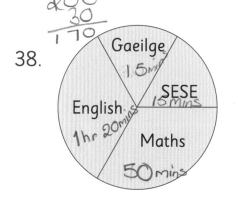

This pie chart shows the amount of time Caroline spent on 4 subjects for homework one night last week. If she spent 2 hours doing homework, how long did she spend doing SESE? _15mins_ S65

39. This grid shows the temperature at Cork Airport during a week in October.

Days	M	T	W	Th	F	S	S
°C	10	9	8	5	6	7	4

(a) Calculate the average temperature. _____ S66

(b) On how many days was the temperature below average? _____ S67

Number of skills mastered ⬜/40

Sixth Class

1. Write the following numbers in order, beginning with the largest. S3
   256.96, 265.96, 295.66, 256.66 _____, _____, _____, _____

2. Round 75.586 to 1 decimal place. _____ S4

3. Add 3561.28 and 869.967. _____ S5

4. 3641.29 – 867.596 = _____ S6

5. 3.874 x 8 = _____ S7   6. 8820 ÷ 36 = _____ S8

7. This shopkeeper bought 27 boxes of nuts for Hallowe'en.
   There were 24 packs in each box.
   How many packs were there altogether? _____ S10

8. Write $\frac{23}{6}$ as a mixed number. _____ S14

9. True or false? $3\frac{3}{7} = \frac{24}{7}$ T ☐ F ☐ S15

10. Write $\frac{1}{3}$ in the correct place on this part of the number line.

S16

0        $\frac{1}{9}$ $\frac{7}{9}$ 1

11. What fraction of 25 is 10? _____ S17

12. $2\frac{3}{5} + 1\frac{1}{2}$ = _____ S18   13. $3\frac{1}{2} - 1\frac{5}{6}$ = _____ S19

14. $\frac{7}{10} \times \frac{5}{8}$ = _____ S20

15. $4 \div \frac{1}{5}$ = _____ S21

16. 24 sweets were divided between 2 children, Tom and Gerry, in the ratio of 5:3. How many sweets did Gerry get? _____

17. Write 45% as a fraction. _____   18. 0.09 = _____%

19. A garage owner bought a car for €12 500. When he sold it he made a profit of 20%. What was the selling price of the car? _____

20. True or false? 91 is a prime number. T ☐ F ☐

21. Find the highest common factor of 24 and 56. ____ S30

22. Circle the common multiple of 9 and 12 in this list.
18, 24, 27, 36, 45, 48 S31

23. Which of the following is the square root of 64? 27, 9, 3, 8 ____ S32

24. Fill in the missing number on this part of the number line.

⁻3   ⁻2   ___   0   1   2   3   4   5   S34

25. Use the number line in the previous question to find the answer to this question. ⁺5 + ⁻6 = ____ S35

26. 6 + 8 x 2 ÷ 4 − 6 = ____ S36

27. Change this word problem into a number sentence and find the missing number. I thought of a number. I added 8 to it and my answer was 15. What number did I think of? (Use c for the missing number.)

_____, c = ____ S37

28. Find the value of b if 2b + 7 = 19. b = ____ S38

29. In this box, construct a triangle with 2 sides measuring 5cm and 3cm with an angle of 100° between them. S41

30. Mark the point with co-ordinates (3, 4) on this grid. S44

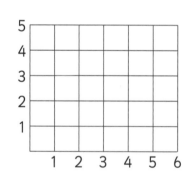

31. B   Tick the correct box.
Angle B is (a) acute ☐   (b) straight ☐
(c) obtuse ☐   (d) reflex ☐.   S47

32. A   Find the measure of angle A in degrees.
∠A = ____° S48

33. In this box, construct an angle of 75°.

34. 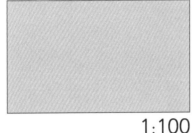 Look at this scale drawing of a garden.
The scale used is 1:100.
Find the actual length of the garden. _____m

1:100

35. 2kg 750g = 2 ☐ kg

You may use a calculator for Questions 36 and 37.

36. If €1 = £0.63 sterling, find the value of €35 in sterling. £_____ sterling

37. If €1 is equal to US$1.05, find the value of US$21 in euro. €_____

Number of skills mastered /37

1. Write these numbers in order, starting with the largest.
   30.078, 30.807, 30.708 _____, _____, _____ S3

2. Round 67.385 to 2 decimal places. _____ S4

3. 302.7 + 5.96 + 17.538 = _____ S5   4. 58 – 29.763 = _____ S6

5. 6.687 x 9 = _____ S7   6. 1015 ÷ 35 = _____ S8

7. 2.52 ÷ 0.28 = _____ S9

8. This box of chocolates contains 56 sweets. How many boxes  like this one are needed to hold 1288 sweets? _____ S10

9. $\frac{22}{5}$ = ___ $\boxed{}$ S14   10. $3\frac{3}{8}$ = $\boxed{}$ S15

11. Write $2\frac{1}{6}$ in the correct place on this part of the number line.

 S16

12. 12 is $\boxed{}$ of 72. S17   13. $2\frac{3}{4} + 1\frac{7}{12}$ = ___ $\boxed{}$ S18

14. $4\frac{1}{4} - 2\frac{2}{3}$ = ___ $\boxed{}$ S19   15. $\frac{3}{4} \times \frac{1}{3}$ = $\boxed{}$ S20

16. $5 \div \frac{1}{3}$ = ___ S21

17. A prize of €35 was divided between 2 people in the ratio of 3:2. How much did each person receive? _____, _____ S22

18. 65% = $\boxed{}$ S23   19. 0.05 = ____% S24

20. How much will this television cost? _____

21. Write the prime number that is greater than 50 and less than 55. ____

22. Find the highest common factor of 12, 20 and 28. ____

23. Find the lowest common multiple of 7 and 5. ____

24. 12 is the square root of _____.

25. Write ⁻7 in the correct place on this part of the number line.

3

26. ⁻5 + ⁻4 = _____   27. 90 ÷ 10 + (6 x 5) − 19 = _____

28. Write an equation for this word problem and find the answer.
Stephen keyed in a certain number on his calculator. He divided it
by 4 and the answer was 19. What number did he key into his
calculator at first? (Use c for the missing number.) _____, c = _____

29. Find the value of y in this equation. 8y − 13 = 75 y = _____

30. In this box, construct a triangle in
which 2 of the angles measure 60°
each and 1 side measures 3.5cm.

31. Write down the co-ordinates of point A. _____ (S44)

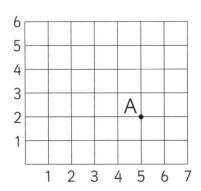

32.  Name this shape. _____ (S45)

33. Draw the net of a tetrahedron in this box. (S46)

34. 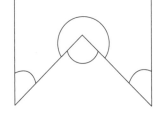 Shade in the reflex angle in this shape. (S47)

35. Measure ∠A in this triangle. ∠A = _____° (S48)

36. Construct an angle of 130° in this box. (S49)

37.  This is a scale drawing of a kitchen. In reality, how much longer is the kitchen than it is wide? _____m (S53)

1:100

20

38. Find the area of this shape. _____cm²

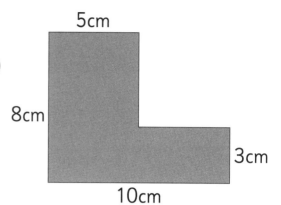

39.  Find the area of this playground in ares. _____

40. Find the surface area of this cube with edges 2cm in length. _____cm²

41. This is a scale plan of a large table. The scale used is 1:100. Find the actual area of the table. _____m²

1:100

42. $4\frac{4}{5}l$ = ___l _____ml

43. The time in Los Angeles is 8 hours behind the time in Dublin. What time is it in Los Angeles when it is 13:30 in Dublin? ____:____

44. A driver drove for 2 hours 15 minutes at an average speed of 60km/h. How far did she travel? _____km

You may use a calculator for Questions 45 and 46.

45. €650 = _____ Australian dollars S62

Euro Exchange Rates	
Currency	Euro value
Australian dollar	1.8
Canadian dollar	1.5

46. $825 Canadian dollars = €_____ S63

47. This bag contains 1 of each of the following coins: 1c, 2c, 5c, 10c and 20c. John asked his friend Jessica to draw out 2 coins without looking in the bag. He then asked her to write down all the possible amounts of money she could pick out. Here is what she wrote:

3c, 6c, 7c, 11c, 12c, 14c, 15c, 21c, 22c, 25c, 30c.

Circle the amount that Jessica could not have picked out of the bag. S68

48. This time John asked Alan to choose 1 cube (without looking inside the bag) from a bag containing 6 red cubes, 4 green cubes and 2 yellow cubes. Mark the probability of the following on the scale by putting an X in the correct place.

Alan will pick out a cube that is not red.

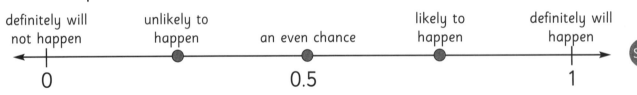

definitely will not happen — unlikely to happen — an even chance — likely to happen — definitely will happen S69

0   0.5   1

49. Rebecca tossed 2 coins 50 times and recorded the outcome here. Fill in the missing information in the grid and then answer this question.

	Outcome	Tally	Frequency
(a)	2 tails	IIII IIII IIII	
(b)	2 heads		
(c)	1 head, 1 tail		21

How many more times did outcome (c) occur than outcome (b)? _____ S70

Number of skills mastered   /49

Mental Assessment

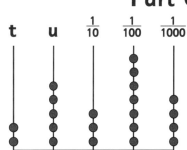

1. Write down the number shown on this abacus.
   _____

2. Write down this number.
   Fifty-six point three eight. _____

3. True or false? 6.08 < 6.8 T ☐ F ☐

4. Round 8.594 to the nearest whole number. ____

5. 3.74 + 2.25 = ____

6. 9.98 – 2.86 = ____

7. 2.76 x 3 = _____

8. 2.8 ÷ 0.4 = ____

9. 132 ÷ 11 = ____

10. Find the cost of 8 apples at 26c each. _____

11. By how much is 96 bigger than 49? _____

12. Michael thought of a number. He multiplied it by 7 and his answer was 8.4. What number did he think of? _____

13. Find the missing number. $\dfrac{2}{\boxed{}} = \dfrac{6}{15}$

14. True or false? $\dfrac{3}{4} < \dfrac{5}{8}$ T ☐ F ☐

15. Put in the correct sign <, = or > between this pair of fractions. $\dfrac{1}{2}$ ☐ $\dfrac{2}{5}$

16. Write $3\dfrac{7}{100}$ in decimal form. _____

17. Write $\dfrac{13}{4}$ as a mixed number. _____

18. Write $3\dfrac{1}{5}$ as an improper fraction. _____

19. Shade in the circle where $\dfrac{3}{5}$ should be on this part of the number line.

0 ———○———○———○———○———○———○———○———○———○——— 1

23

20. What fraction of 30 is 10? _____

21. $\frac{1}{3} + \frac{1}{4} =$ ___

22. $1\frac{1}{2} + \frac{3}{4} =$ ___

23. $\frac{5}{6} - \frac{1}{3} =$ ___

24. $\frac{1}{2} - \frac{1}{5} =$ ___

25. $\frac{1}{3} \times 9 =$ ___

26. $\frac{1}{2} \times \frac{1}{5} =$ ___

27. $4 \div \frac{1}{3} =$ ___

28. $3 \div \frac{1}{5} =$ ___

29. Divide €72 between Michael and James in the ratio of 5:1. How much does Michael get? _____

30. $\frac{3}{4} =$ _____%

31. $\dfrac{2}{\boxed{}} = 40\%$

32. $12\frac{1}{2}\% = \dfrac{\boxed{}}{\boxed{}}$

33. Write 0.6 as a percentage. _____%

34. Put these in order, starting with the biggest.
$\frac{3}{4}$, 70%, 0.76, $\frac{3}{5}$ _____, _____, _____, _____

35. By how much is 20% of 35 bigger than 25% of 24? _____

36. Write down the factors of 67. _____

37. Find the factors of 18. _____

38. Find the highest common factor of 32 and 40. _____

39. Write down the first 3 multiples of 15. _____, _____, _____

40. What is the lowest common multiple of 10 and 12? _____

41. Which of these is not a square number? 16, 25, 1, 60, 81 _____

42. Write down the square root of 144. _____

43. True or false? $81 = 8^2$ T ☐ F ☐

44. Use the number line to find the value of $^+5 + {}^-4$. _____

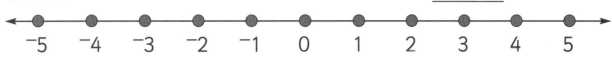

-5   -4   -3   -2   -1   0   1   2   3   4   5

45. By how much is $^-3$ less than $^+4$? _____

46. The temperature in Moscow was $^+3°$ at noon.
By midnight it had fallen by 8 degrees.
What was the temperature then? _____ °

47.  €60 These runners were reduced by 20% in the sales.
What was the sale price? _____

48. This TV was priced at €250 before VAT of 20% was
added on. What was the selling price of the TV? _____

49.  Joseph had 80 football cards but lost 26 of them.
How many did he have left? _____

50. If these 6 buns cost €1.50, how much is each bun? _____

Part One: Number of skills mastered ⬜/50

51. Round 157.502 to the nearest whole number. _____

52. 13.2 + 18.94 = _____   53. 19.28 – 7.45 = _____   54. 4.58 x 5 = _____

55. 5.6 ÷ 0.7 = _____   56. $\frac{2}{3} + \frac{1}{4}$ = _____   57. $\frac{3}{4} - \frac{5}{8}$ = _____

58. $\frac{2}{5}$ x 8 = _____   59. 4 ÷ $\frac{1}{7}$ = _____

60. Find the odd one out. F32 = (1, 2, 4, 9, 16, 32) _____

61. Write down the factors of 101. _____

62. True or false? The multiple of 12 nearest to 100 is 98. T ☐ F ☐

63. What is the lowest common multiple of 11 and 5? _____

64. 6 x 9 – 18 ÷ 3 + 6 = _____   65. 12 + 8 x 6 ÷ 4 – 9 = _____

66. 40 – 30 ÷ 5 x 2 + 19 = _____

Find the value of a in each of the following equations.
67. 3a + 2 = 11   a = _____   68. 5a – 8 = 17   a = _____

69. 7a – 6 = 22   a = _____   70. Which of the following could not be
                                   the measure of angle A?
                                   120° ☐ 60° ☐ 130° ☐

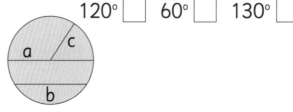

71. Which of the lines a, b or c is
    the radius of this circle? _____

72. Which of the following is an isosceles triangle? Tick the correct box.
(a)   (b)   (c)   (d)

 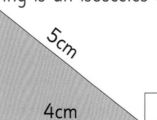 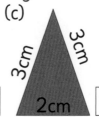

26

Find the size of the missing angle in each of the following without using a protractor.

73.  ∠C = ____ °

74. 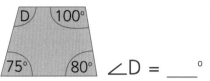 ∠D = ____ °

75. 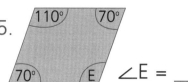 ∠E = ____ °

76. Write $2\frac{1}{4}$ kg as grammes. _____ g

77. How many millilitres is 2.006 litres? _____ ml

78. How many metres are in $3\frac{1}{5}$ kilometres? _____ m

Find the perimeter of each of the following shapes.

79. 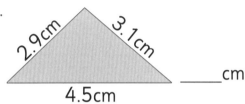 _____ cm

80. 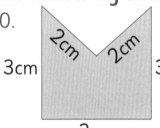 _____ cm

81. Find the perimeter of a rhombus with sides 6.5cm long. _____ cm

82. Find the actual perimeter of this field in metres. _____ m

1:100

Fill in the missing 24-hour times on these clocks.

83.

9:30 a.m.

84.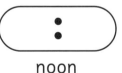

noon

85.

11:15 p.m.

86. If €1 is worth £0.63 sterling, find the value of €5 in sterling. _____

87. It is approximately 160km from Boyle to Dublin. If a lorry travels at an average speed of 40km per hour, how long will the journey take? _____

88.  A car travelled the 175 kilometres from Tuam to Cork in 5 hours. What was the car's average speed per hour? _____

89. Find the average of 8, 12 and 16. _____

90. The average of 3 numbers (3, a and 5) is 4. Find the value of a. _____

Find the areas of the following quadrilaterals.

91.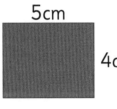
5cm
4cm

Area = _____cm²

92.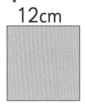
12cm

Area = _____cm²

93.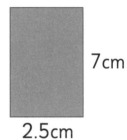
7cm
2.5cm

Area = _____cm²

94. Find the area of a square field with sides 20 metres long. _____m²

95.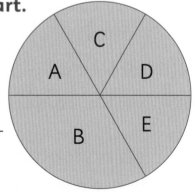
Area = 96cm²   8cm

Find the length of this rectangle._____cm

96. If the perimeter of a square page is 44cm, find the area of the page. _____cm²

97. What is the second-highest possible score when 3 dice are thrown? _____

98. What are the chances of getting an even number when 1 dice is rolled? ☐ in ☐

Answer the following questions based on this pie chart.

99. If section A represents 16 children, how many children are represented in section B? _____

100. How many children are represented altogether? _____

Part Two: Skills mastered /50

Total number of skills mastered
(Part One and Part Two) /100

End of Year Assessment*   **Part One**

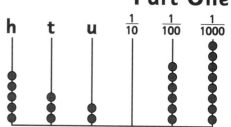

1. Which of the underlined digits has the greater value? 35.<u>7</u>6<u>8</u> ____

2. Write the number shown on this abacus. _____

3. Write these numbers in order, starting with the smallest.
   79.634, 79.346, 79.436, 79.364 _____, _____, _____, _____

4. Round 60.449 to 1 decimal place. _____

5. $16.9 + 163.764 + 8.53 =$ _____   6. $97.32 - 68.685 =$ _____

7. $7.546 \times 8 =$ _____   8. $1702 \div 46 =$ _____   9. $4.75 \div 0.19 =$ _____

10. Claire's grandmother was born in 1936. What age is her grandmother now? _____

11. Put a tick in the box beside the correct answer.
    $\frac{5}{6} =$ (a) $\frac{2}{3}$ ☐ (b) $\frac{3}{4}$ ☐ (c) $\frac{10}{12}$ ☐

12. Put these fractions in order, starting with the largest.
    $\frac{1}{2}, \frac{3}{8}, \frac{11}{12}, \frac{1}{4}, \frac{7}{8}$ _____, _____, _____, _____, _____

13. $7\frac{207}{1000} =$ ___._____   14. $\frac{32}{9} =$ ___$\boxed{}$ 15. $5\frac{7}{10} =$ $\boxed{}$

16. Write $1\frac{2}{3}$ in the correct place on this part of the number line.

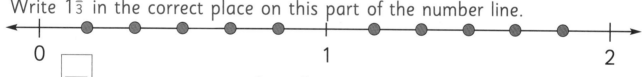

17. 15 is $\boxed{}$ of 60.   18. $6\frac{2}{3} + 3\frac{7}{9} =$ _____   19. $5\frac{1}{8} - 2\frac{3}{4} =$ _____

20. $\frac{1}{5} \times \frac{5}{7} =$ ___   21. $6 \div \frac{1}{4} =$ ___

22. Divide €56 between 2 children in the ratio of 2:5. How much does each child get? _____, _____

23. $12\frac{1}{2}\% =$ ___._____   24. $\frac{3}{5} =$ ____%

* Note to teacher: The questions in this assessment match the Sixth Class skills 1–70, i.e. Question 1 tests Skill 1, Question 2 tests Skill 2 and so on.

29

25. Aideen spent 10% of her €5.50 and Paul spent 20% of his €3.
    How much more than Aideen did Paul spend? _____

26. 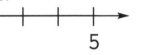 The price of this jacket was reduced by 30% in a sale.
    What was the sale price of the jacket? _____

27. How many prime numbers are there in this square? _____

27	48	71
97	3	93
14	51	1

28. List the composite numbers greater than 35 and less than 40. _____

29. Write the first square number greater than 50. _____

30. List the common factors of 14 and 35. _____

31. What is the lowest common multiple of 10 and 14? _____

32. True or false? $\sqrt{169}$ = 14 T ☐ F ☐   33. True or false? 36 = 5^2 T ☐ F ☐

34. Write ⁻9 in the correct place on this part of the number line.

    ⟵—+—+—+—+—+—+—+—+—+—+—+—+—+—+—+—+—+—⟶
                                                          5

35. What is the difference in temperature between ⁺5°C and ⁻4°C? _____°C

36. 24 x 3 ÷ 9 + 15 = _____

37. Write a number sentence to match this word problem  and find the answer. When Lisa bought this CD she had €24.65 left. How much money did she have at first? _____

38. $\frac{63}{a}$ = 9 a = _____

39. True or false? A right-angled triangle can have 2 acute angles measuring 55° and 45°. T ☐ F ☐

40. Write in the missing number. All quadrilaterals have _____ angles.

Part One: Number of skills mastered ⬜ 40

41. In the box, construct a triangle in which 2 angles measure 70° each and 1 side measures 3cm.

42. Name the coloured part of this circle. _____

43. 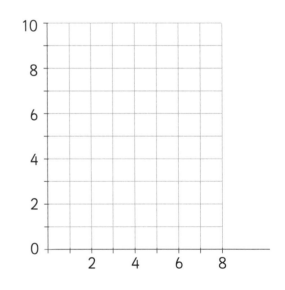 Draw a circle with a radius of 2.5cm in this box.

44. Draw in and name the following points on this grid. A (1, 1), B (1, 9), C (4, 6), D (7, 9), E (7, 1). Use a ruler and pencil to join A to B, B to C, C to D and D to E. What capital letter have you drawn? _____

45. 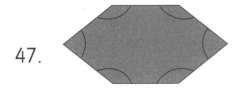 Name this shape. _____

46. Draw the net of a triangular prism in this box.

47. How many acute angles are there in this shape? _____

31

48. Use a protractor to measure angle A. ∠A = _____°

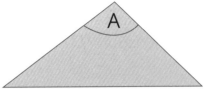

49.

In this box, construct an angle of 35°.

50. The sum of angles A, B and C = 300°. Without using a protractor, find the measure of angle D. ∠D = ___°

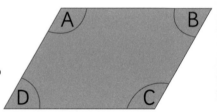

51. 3.05km = ___km ___m

52. Measure the perimeter of this shape. _____cm

53. This is a scale drawing of a classroom. Find the actual perimeter of the room. _____m

1:100

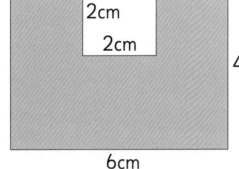

2cm

2cm

4.5cm

54.

Find the area of this shape. _____cm²

6cm

55. Find the area in hectares of a building site 200m in length and 100m in width. _____ hectares

56. 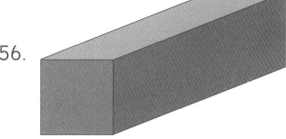 Find the surface area of this cuboid. _____

57. This is a scale drawing of a bedroom. Find the actual area of the room. _____

1:50

58. 10g = ____._____kg   59. 8.065l = __l ___ml

60. The time in New York is 5 hours behind the time in Cork. What time is it in Cork when it is 22:15 in New York? _____

61.  A truck travelled 296km in 4 hours. What was the average speed for the journey? _____

You may use a calculator for Questions 62 and 63.

62. Convert €125 to sterling. £_____ sterling

63. How much is US$495 worth in euro?

€_____

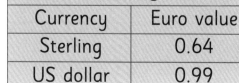

Euro Exchange Rates	
Currency	Euro value
Sterling	0.64
US dollar	0.99

64. This trend graph shows the number of children who visited Cookstown Library during one week. How many more children visited the library on Wednesday than on Saturday? _____

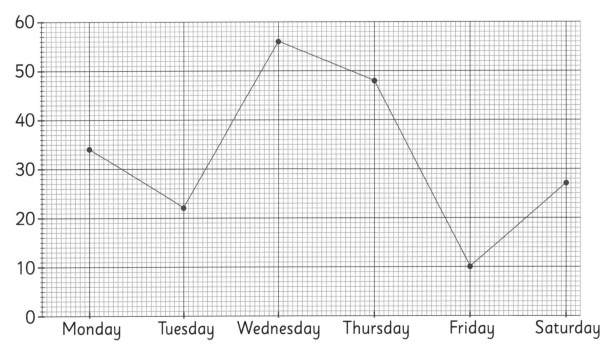

65. This pie chart shows the eye colours of a group of Sixth Class children. 12 children had blue eyes. How many children in the group had grey eyes? _____

66. This grid shows the number of people who attended a theatre over a one-week period. What was the average daily attendance? _____

M	T	W	Th	F	S	S
120	142	108	133	165	160	96

67. On Saturday night 80% of the seats in the theatre were occupied. How many seats are in the theatre? _____

68. These 4 cards are placed face down on a table and you are allowed to pick 2 cards each time and add the 2 numbers for your score. The cards are replaced and moved around after each turn.

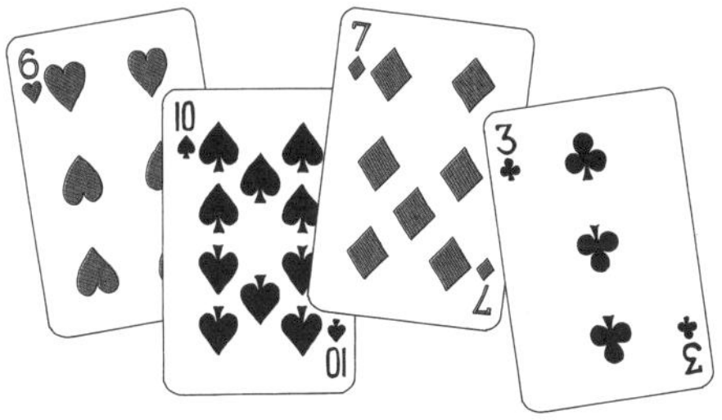

List all the possible totals here. ______________________________

69. Mark the probability of the following on the probability scale by putting an X in the place you choose. Áine is going to California on holiday in July for 3 weeks. It will rain every day while she is there.

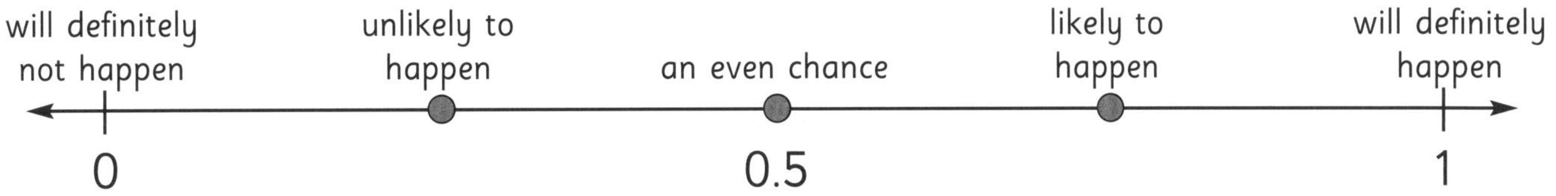
will definitely not happen
unlikely to happen
an even chance
likely to happen
will definitely happen
0
0.5
1

70. Kevin tossed a coin 60 times and recorded the number of times the coin landed on heads and the number of times the coin landed on tails. Fill in the missing information on this grid and then answer the question below.

Outcome	**Tally**	**Frequency**
Heads	𝍸 𝍸 𝍸 𝍸 𝍸 𝍸 III	
Tails		

How many more times did the coin land on heads than on tails? ________

Part Two: Skills mastered ___/30

Total number of skills mastered (Part One and Part Two) ___/70

Sixth Class Beginning of Year Skills Record Sheet

Pupil's name: _Ella Maguire_

See the Fifth Class Skills List in the Solutions Book to cross-reference the skill numbers listed here.

Strand: Number

Place value: ☐1 ☐2 ☐3 ☐4 ☐5

Operations: ☐6 ☐7 ☐8 ☐9 ☐10 ☐11

Fractions: ☐12 ☐13 ☐14 ☐15 ☐16 ☐17 ☐18 ☐19 ☐20

Decimals and percentages: ☐21 ☐22 ☐23 ☐24 ☐25 ☐26

Number theory: ☐27 ☐28 ☐29 ☐30 ☐31 ☐32

Strand: Algebra

Directed numbers: ☐33

Rules and properties: ☐34

Equations: ☐35 ☐36 ☐37

Strand: Shape and space

2-D shapes: ☐38 ☐39 ☐40 ☐41

3-D shapes: ☐42 ☐43

Lines and angles: ☐44 ☐45 ☐46 ☐47

Strand: Measures

Length: ☐48 ☐49

Area: ☐50 ☐51 ☐52

Time: ☐53 ☐54

Money: ☐55 ☐56 ☐57

Strand: Data

Representing and interpreting data: ☐58 ☐59 ☐60 ☐61

Chance: ☐62 ☐63

Skills mastered ◻ 63

Sixth Class Skills Record Sheet

Pupil's name: _Ella Maguire_

Strand: Number

Place value: `1 ☐` `2 ☐` `3 ☐☐☐` `4 ☐☐☐`

Operations: `5 ☐☐☐` `6 ☐☐☐` `7 ☐☐`

`8 ☐☐☐` `9 ☐☐` `10 ☐☐`

Fractions: `11 ☐☐` `12 ☐☐` `13 ☐☐` `14 ☐☐☐` `15 ☐☐☐☐`

`16 ☐☐☐` `17 ☐☐☐` `18 ☐☐☐☐` `19 ☐☐☐☐`

`20 ☐☐` `21 ☐☐` `22 ☐☐`

Decimals and percentages: `23 ☐☐☐` `24 ☐☐☐` `25 ☐☐` `26 ☐☐`

Number theory: `27 ☐☐☐` `28 ☐` `29 ☐` `30 ☐☐☐`

`31 ☐☐☐` `32 ☐☐☐` `33 ☐☐`

Strand: Algebra

Directed numbers: `34 ☐☐` `35 ☐☐`

Rules and properties: `36 ☐` Equations: `37 ☐☐` `38 ☐☐`

Strand: Shape and space

2-D shapes: `39 ☐` `40 ☐` `41 ☐☐☐` `42 ☐` `43 ☐` `44 ☐☐`

3-D shapes: `45 ☐` `46 ☐`

Lines and angles: `47 ☐☐☐` `48 ☐☐☐` `49 ☐☐☐` `50 ☐`

Strand: Measures

Length: `51 ☐` `52 ☐` `53 ☐☐`

Area: `54 ☐` `55 ☐` `56 ☐` `57 ☐`

Weight: `58 ☐` Capacity: `59 ☐` Time: `60 ☐` `61 ☐`

Money: `62 ☐☐☐` `63 ☐☐☐`

Strand: Data

Representing and interpreting data: `64 ☐` `65 ☐` `66 ☐` `67 ☐`

Chance: `68 ☐` `69 ☐` `70 ☐`

Skills mastered ◻/70

38